Bucolia: The Coloring Book

A Pastoral Publication for Relaxation for Our Creative City and Country Cousins

Companion to the Book
Bucolia: Hijinx in the Hinterlands
by Mathew Thuney; Illustrated by Ellen Clark

This book colored by

_____

Welcome to Bucolia!

*"You most likely won't find Bucolia on any map—
but you might just be able to locate it as
a place in your heart."*

Copyright © 2017 by Matthew E. Thuney

All rights reserved. No part of this book may be reproduced or transmitted in any form or by any means, electronic or mechanical, including photocopying, recording or by any information storage and retrieval system, without written permission from the author, except for the inclusion of brief quotations in a review.

Published by
Raven & Frog
P.O. Box 683
Deming, WA 98244
Voice/Text 360.305.6939

For further information please contact the publisher, email the author at bucolia018@gmail.com, or the illustrator magic@magicdraw.net.

Printed in the United States of America.

First Edition Published August 2017.

Also by the author
(available on Amazon.com and through www.facebook.com/Bucolia/)

BUCOLIA: Hijinx in the Hinterlands.
A bewildering, hilarious, heartwarming recollection of the author's misguided attempts to adjust to country living. Sublimely illustrated by Ellen Clark.

ORIGINAL RECIPES:
Tasty Tidbits from "Thuney Casserole" and Other Early Entrees.
What's the recipe for turning a half-baked human into a fully cooked columnist, business owner, and family man? Discover the secret ingredients in this collection of columns, radio scripts, articles, and other assorted nonsense. *Bon appétit!*

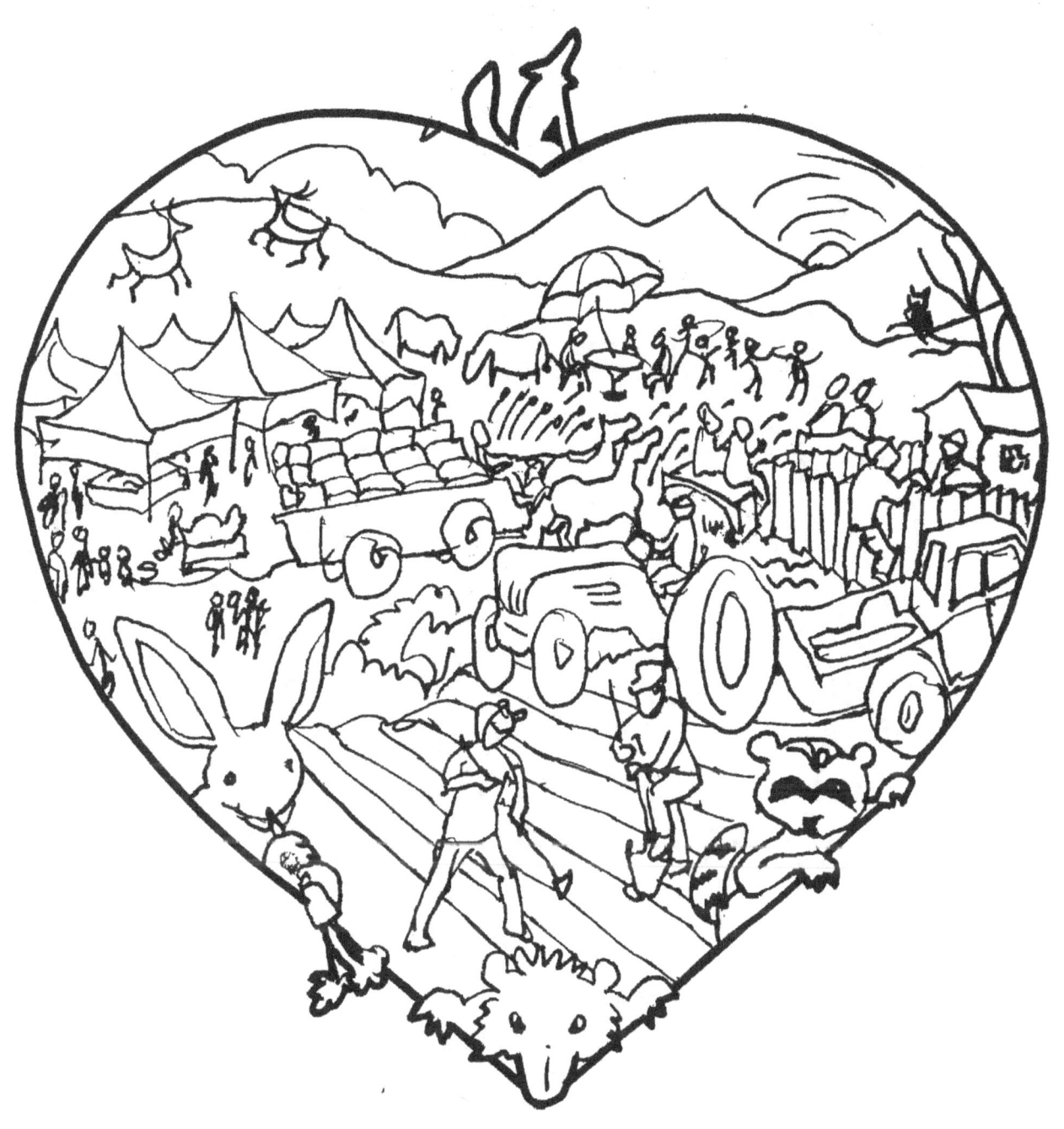

Bucolia

Hijinx in the Hinterlands Coloring Book

A Publication for Relaxation

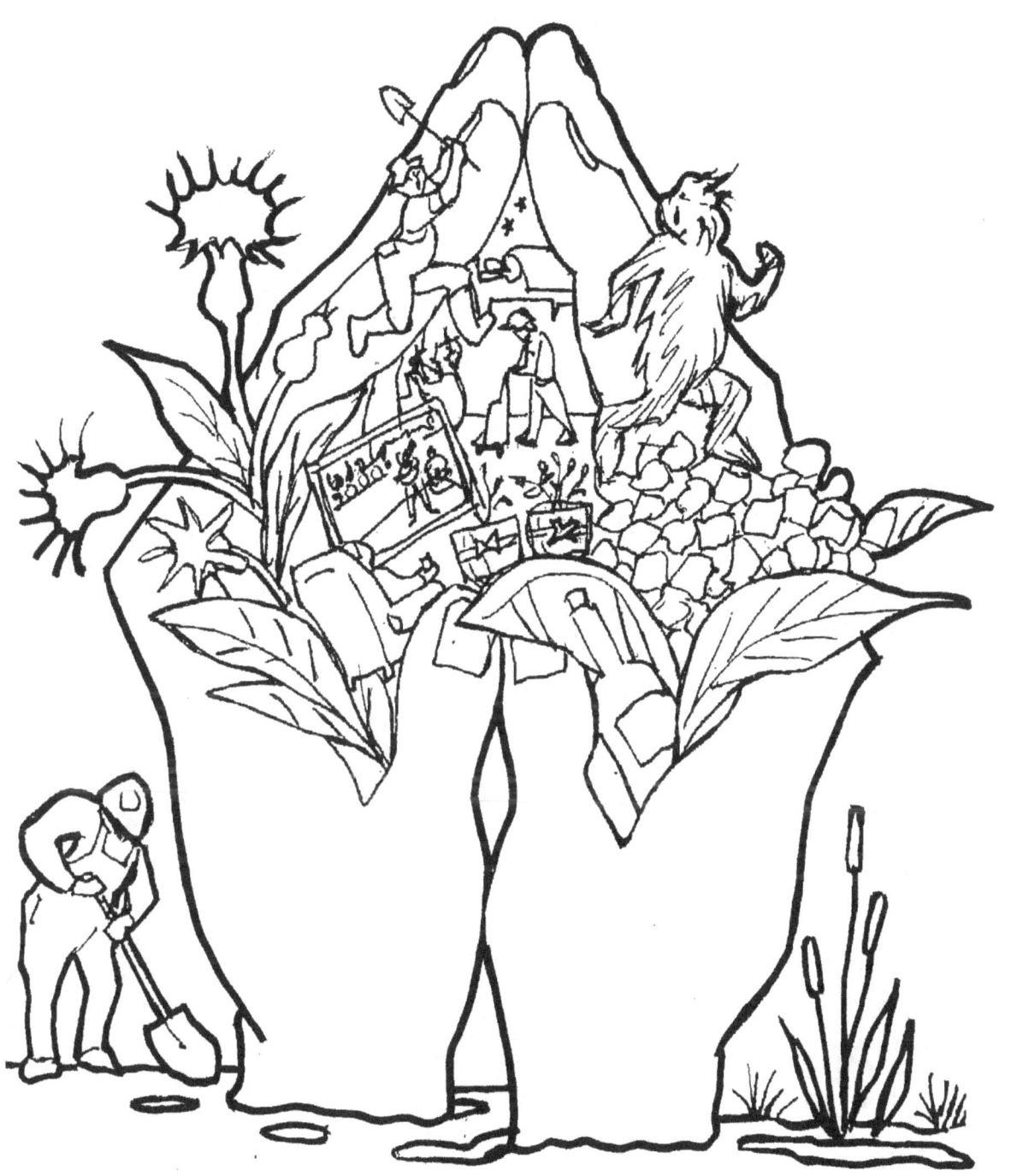

Seeking help for a disgusting, deranged addiction.

"Now that we've moved to the country,
I've begun planting things.
And I can't seem to stop."

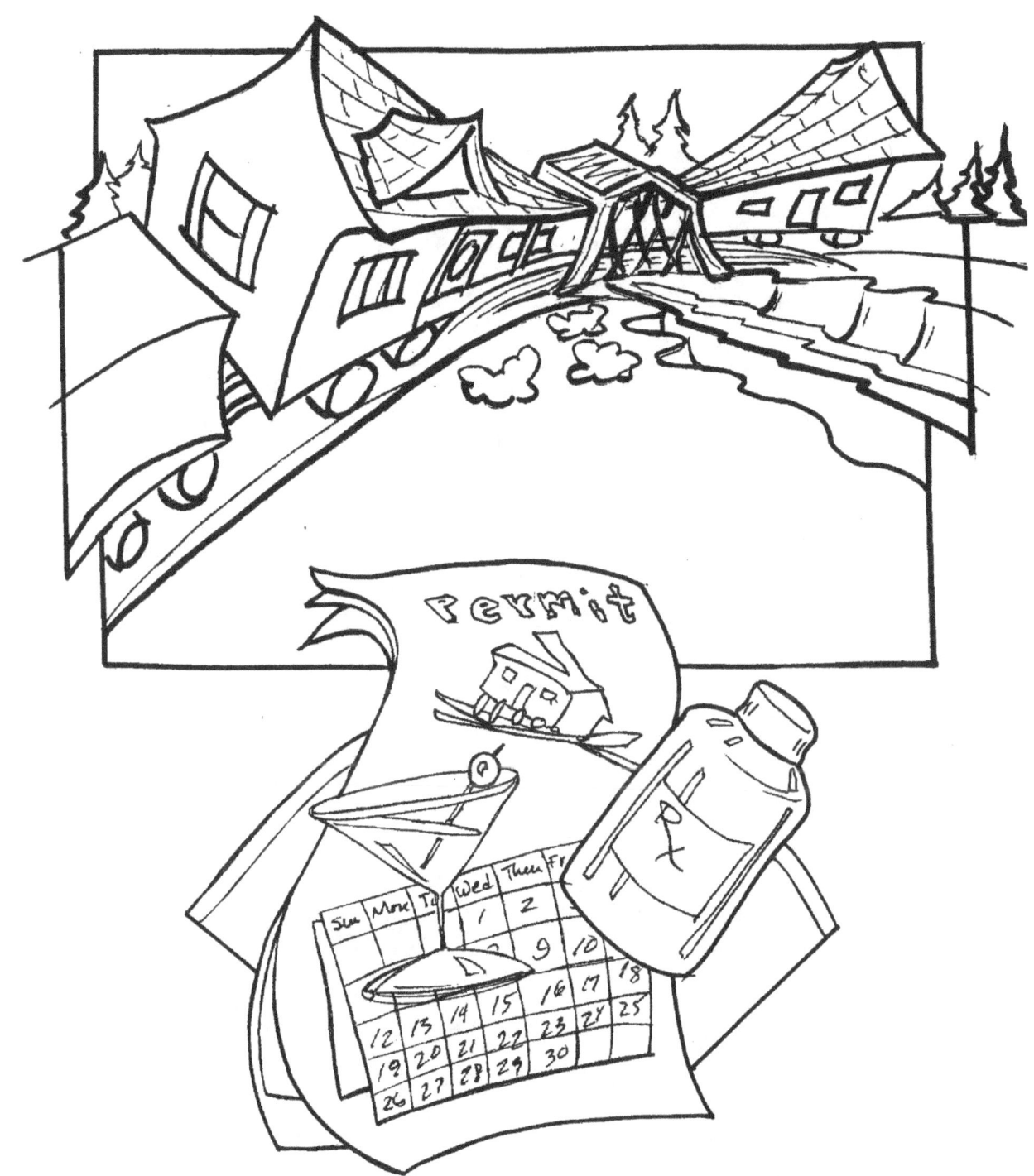

The house that came over the mountain.

"We're SO sorry about the delay in delivering your home. We've encountered one small problem. Were you aware that there's a tiny one-lane bridge that we have to cross?"

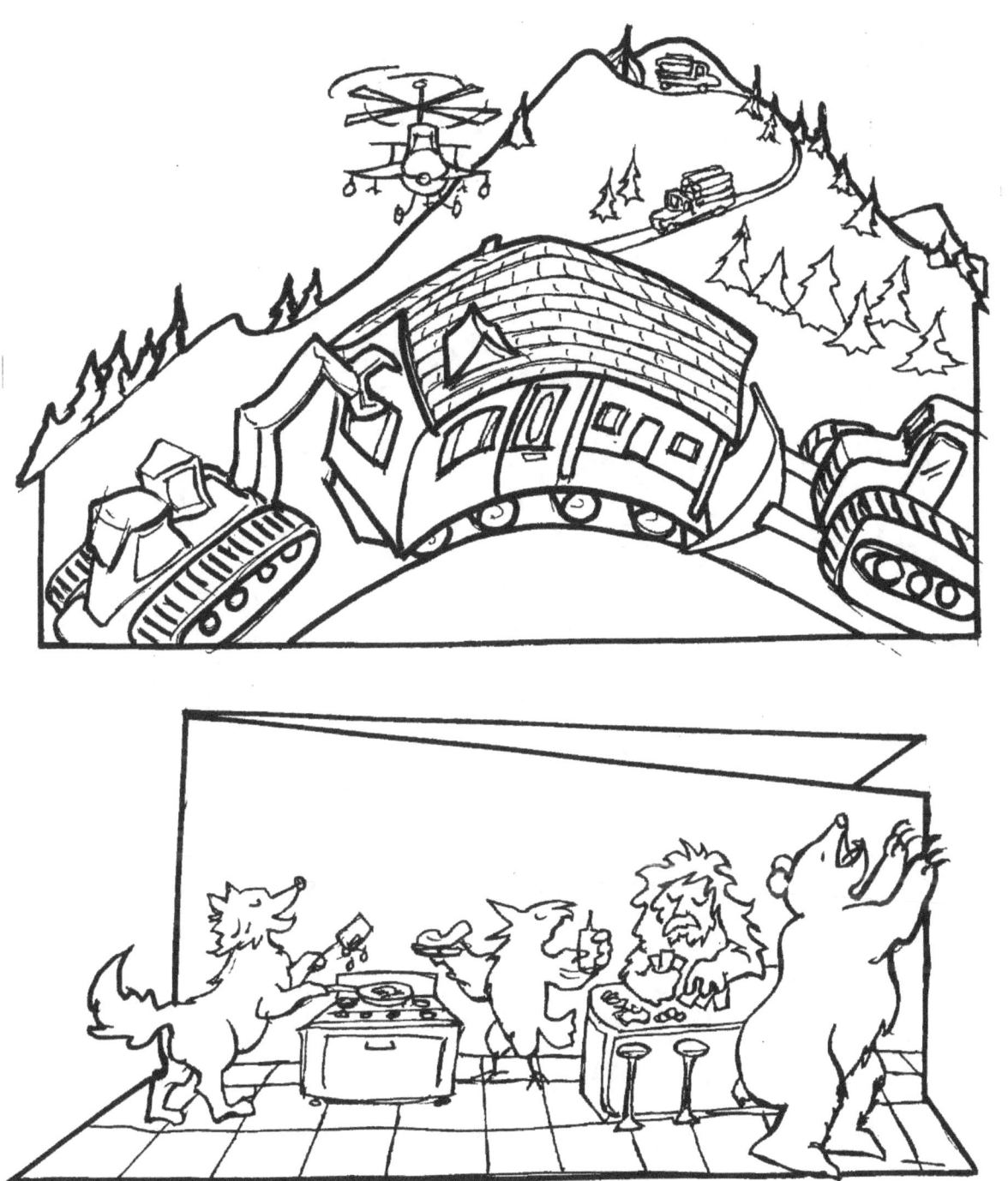

The charge up the mountain.

Woodland creatures making themselves at home
"Your home is parked off to the side of the logging road, safe and sound,
at the very top of the mountain."

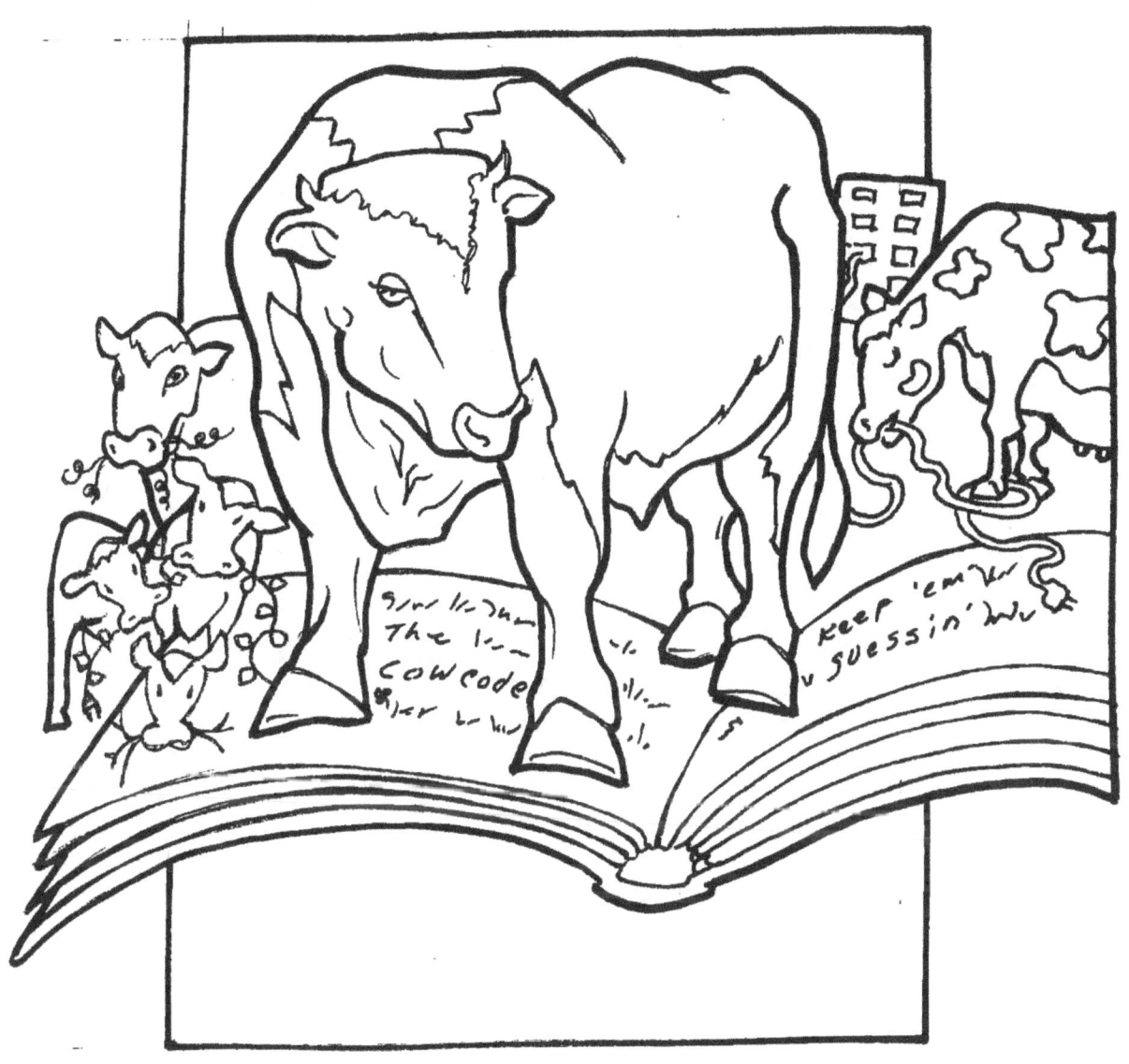

The battle of the hillside.

"That year, this particular herd decided to recruit a Hereford terrorist, a certain wily steer known only by the name Enrique."

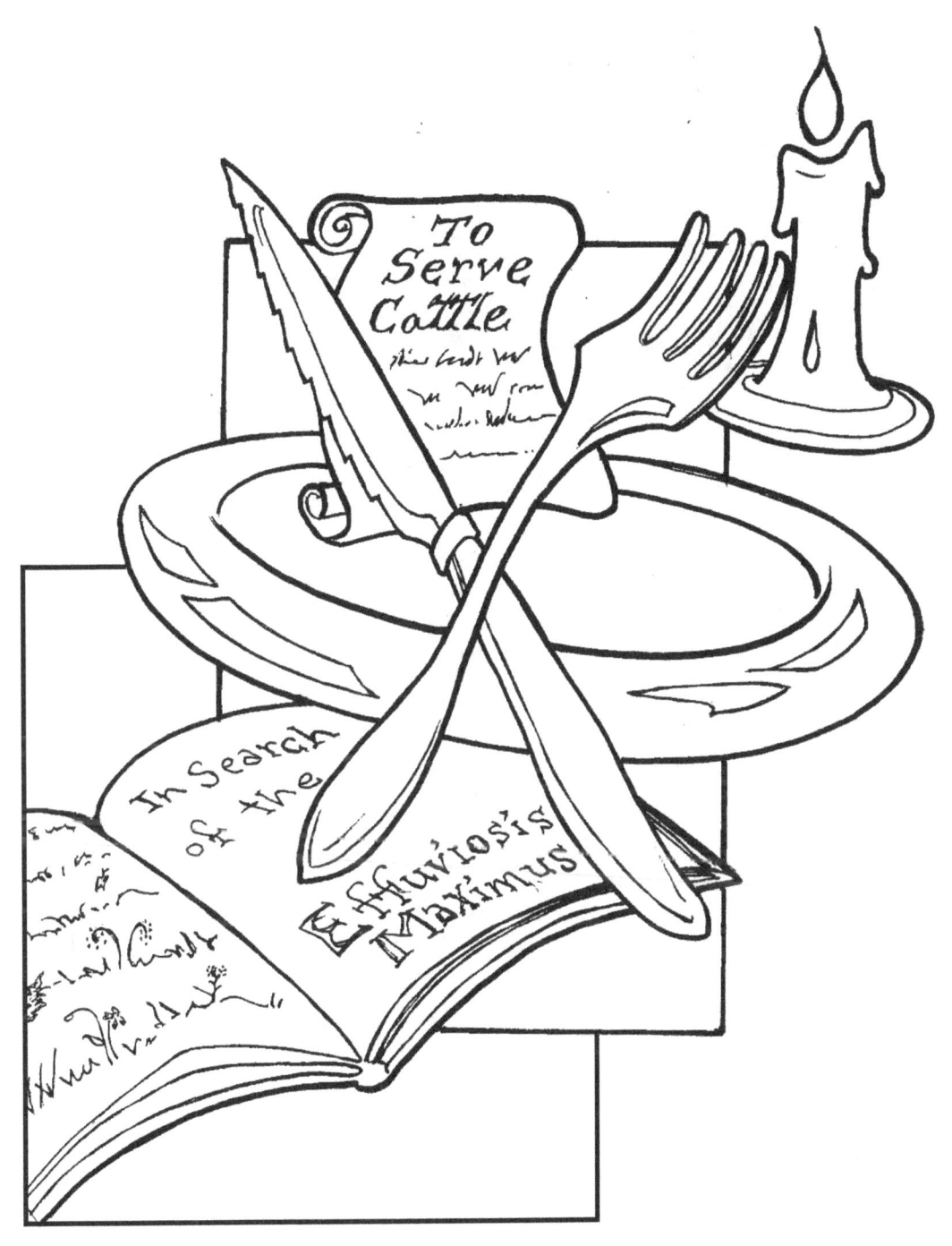

Herdology 101, a city dweller's guide.

"There'll be a quiz on Friday, so don't forget your Blue Books, Merlot, and J.A. Henckels cutlery."

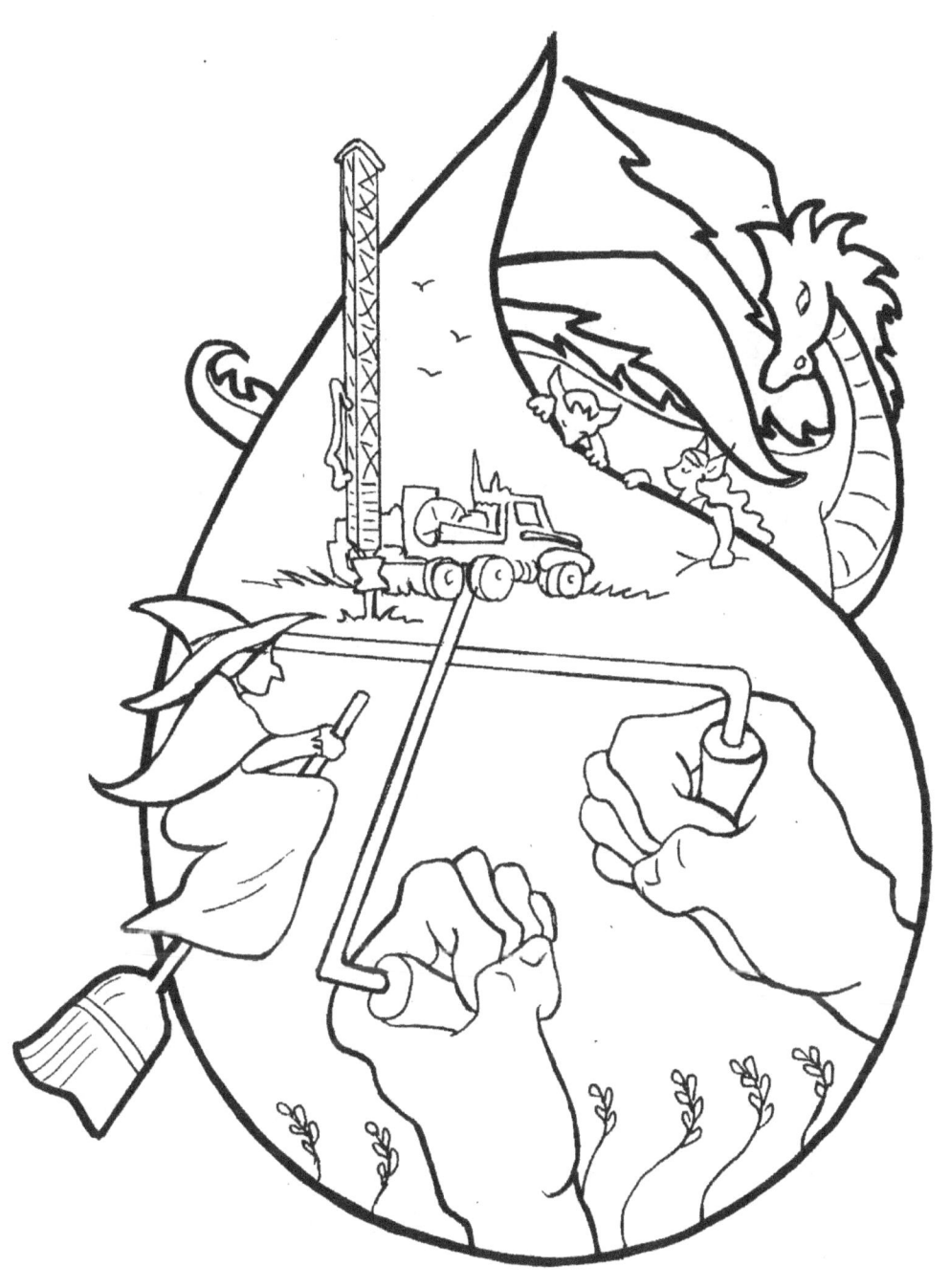

The witching well.

"The witch brought with her a mysterious array of divining devices, but the one she personally used looked like something out of Star Trek. Or more likely Lord of the Rings."

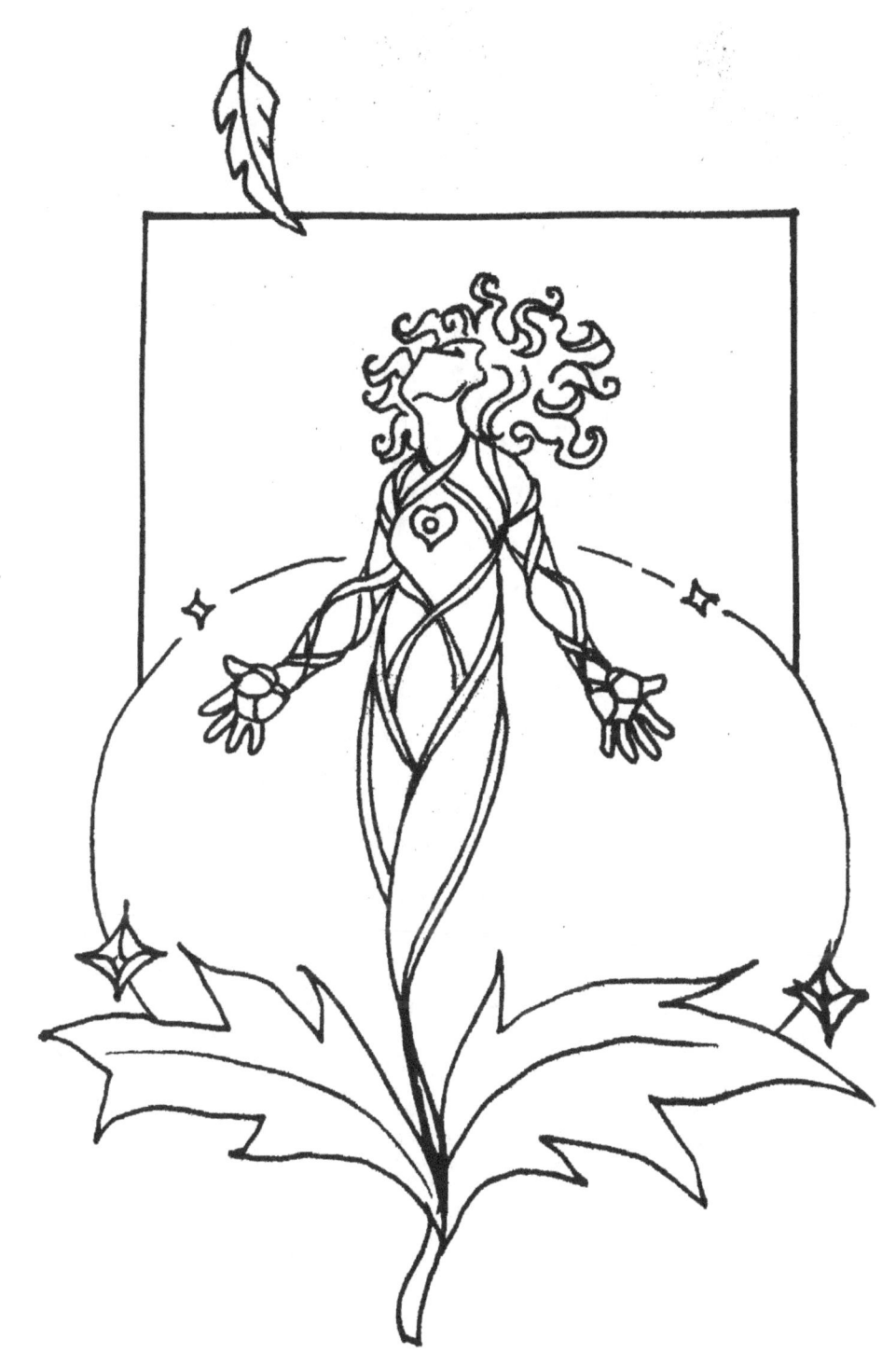

Our magical friend Anna.

"Mystery upon mystery seemed to inhabit and enliven the land."

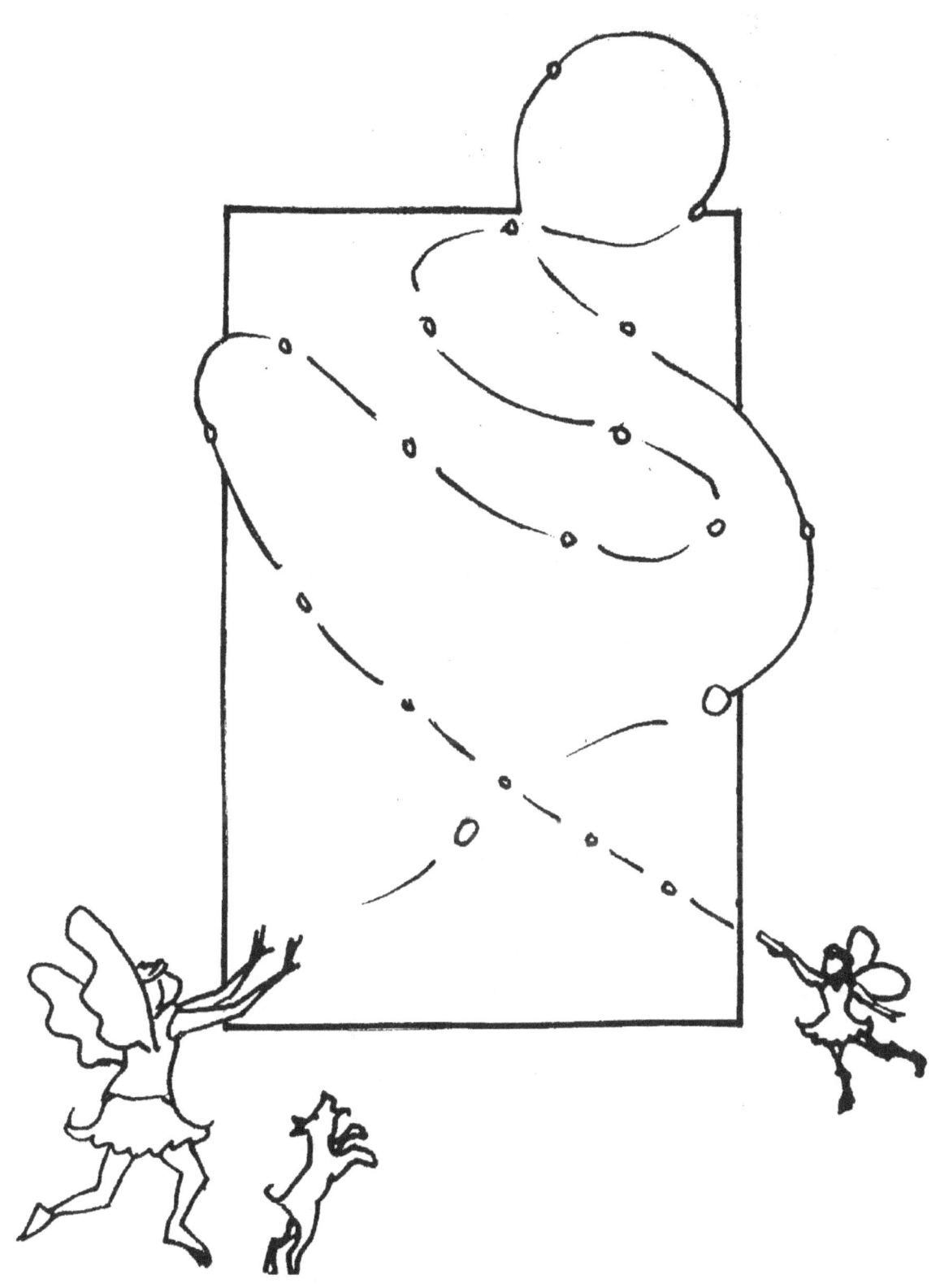

Fairy lights.

"It was a hypnotic vision and we all looked on trying to discern its meaning as the spectacle continued."

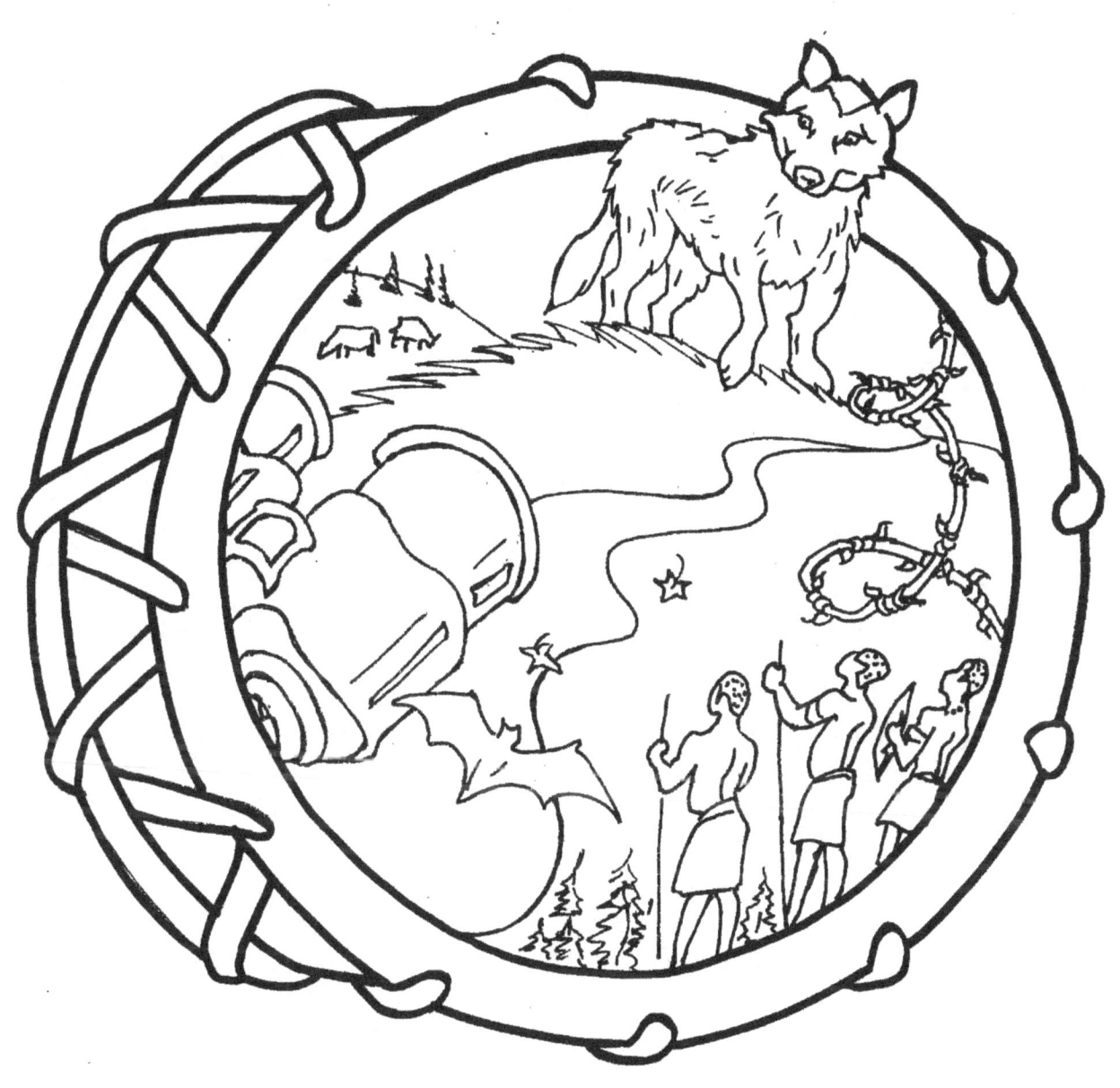

Drumming up a wolf.

"You don't see wolves much anymore, at least not in this corner of Bucolia. It's a real privilege when you do."

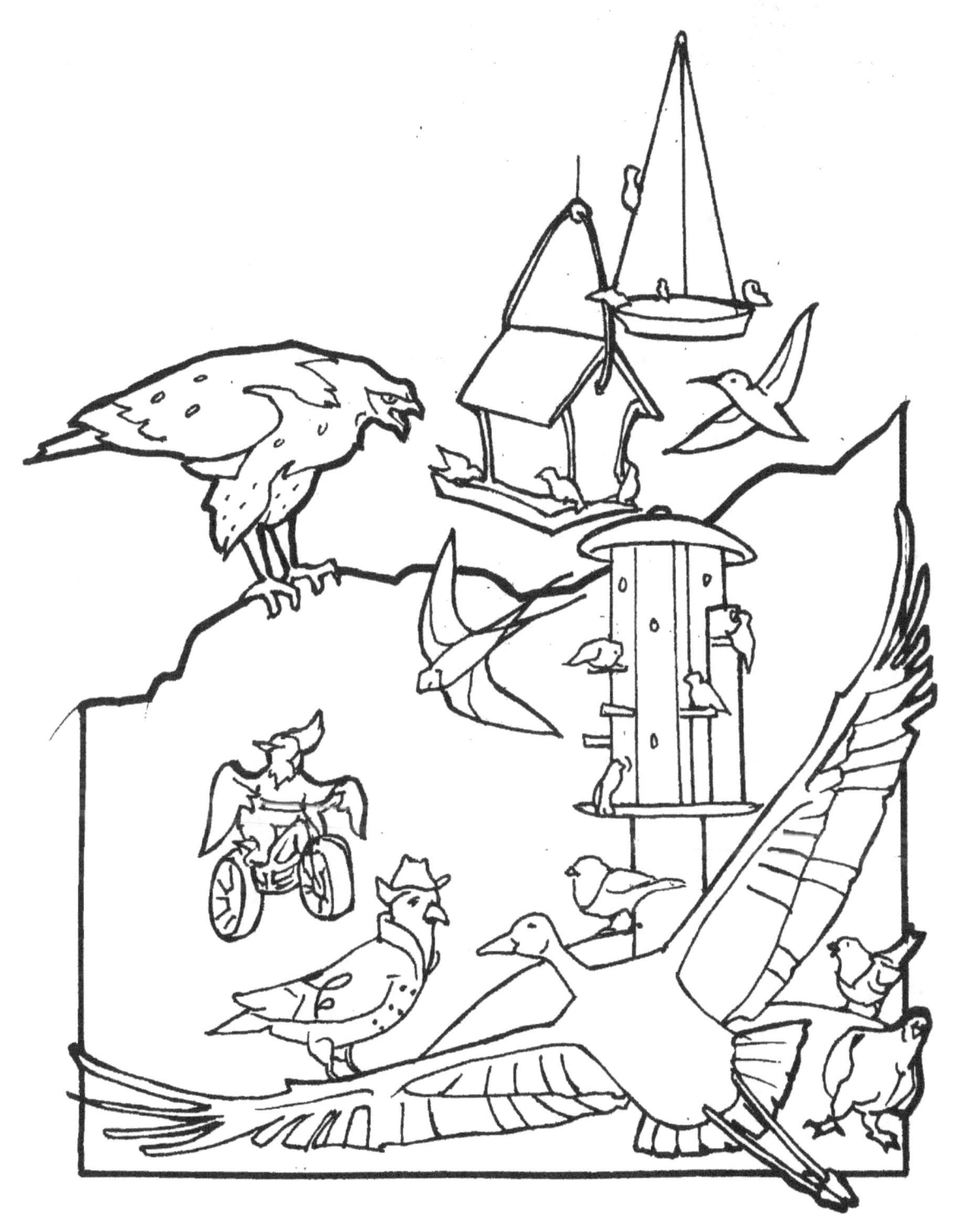

Birds of a feather.

"Watching our amazing avian amigos flutter about and interact has proved to be a constant source of instruction and amusement."

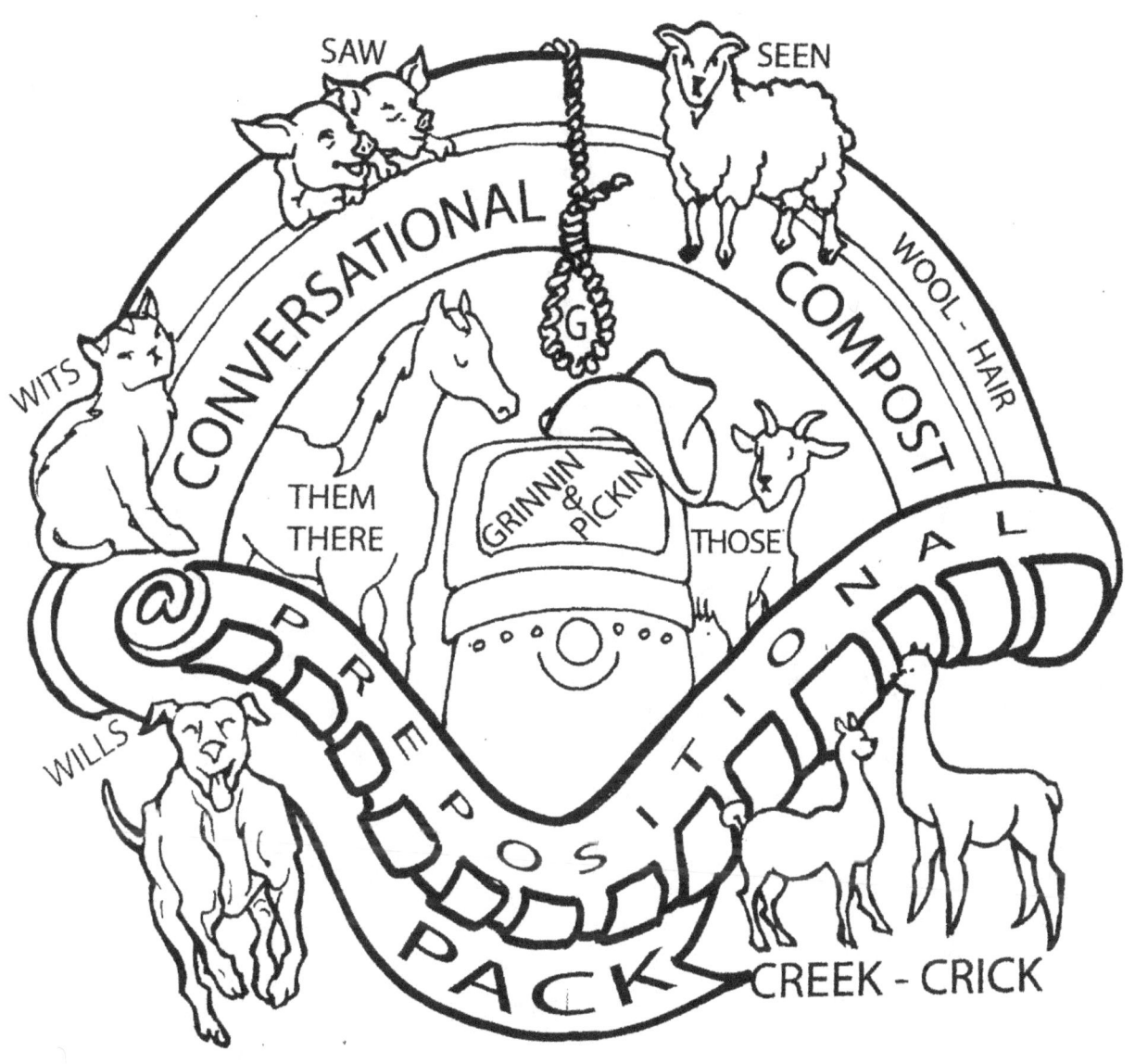

Land of the truncated gerund.

"It's not just the flora and fauna that are colorful in Bucolia. A good part of its charm and spirit come from the two-legged characters that inhabit it."

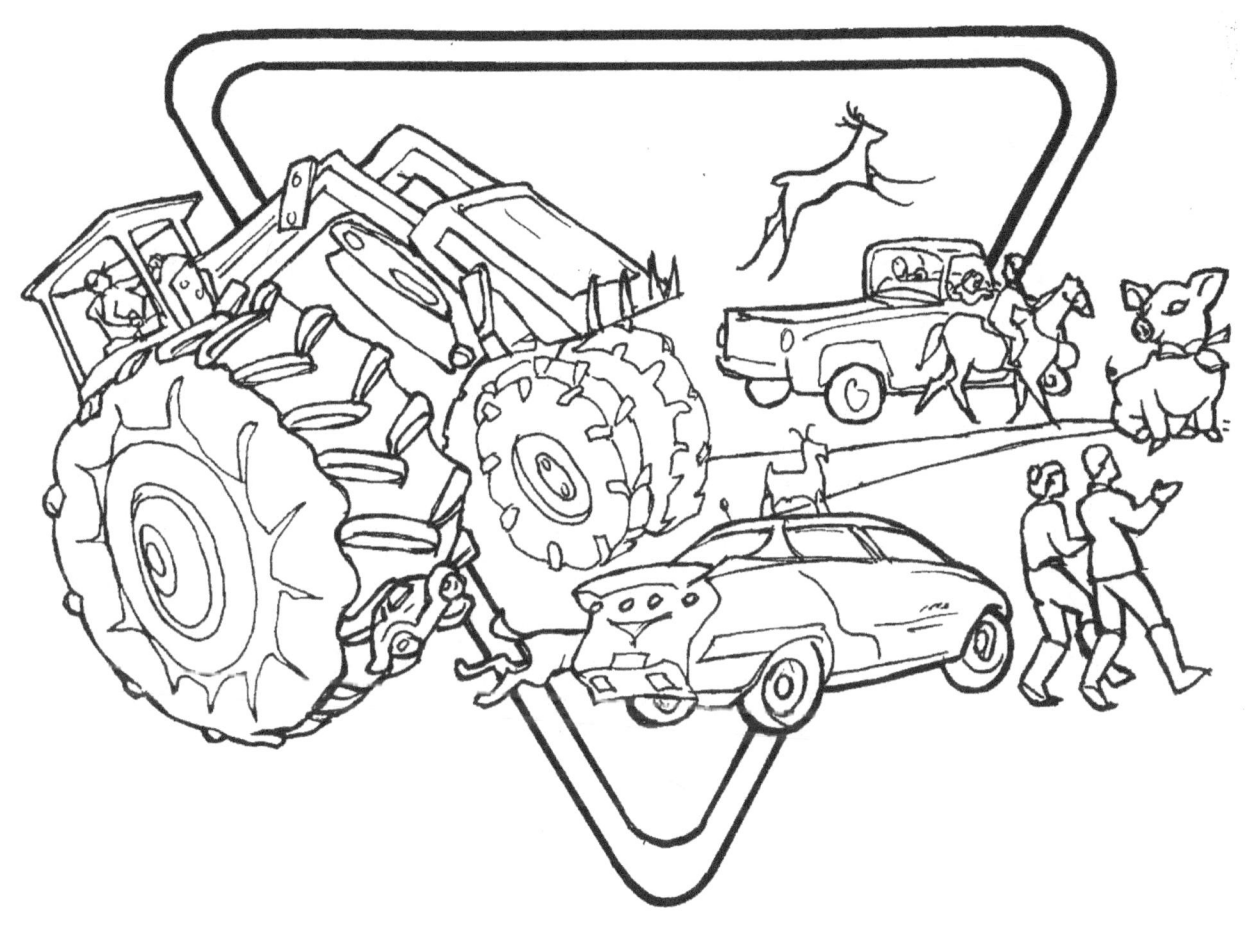

A busy day on the road.

"Talking to neighbors while they walk on the road is Bucolia's version of CNN. It's the best way to get all the news.
And the gossip."

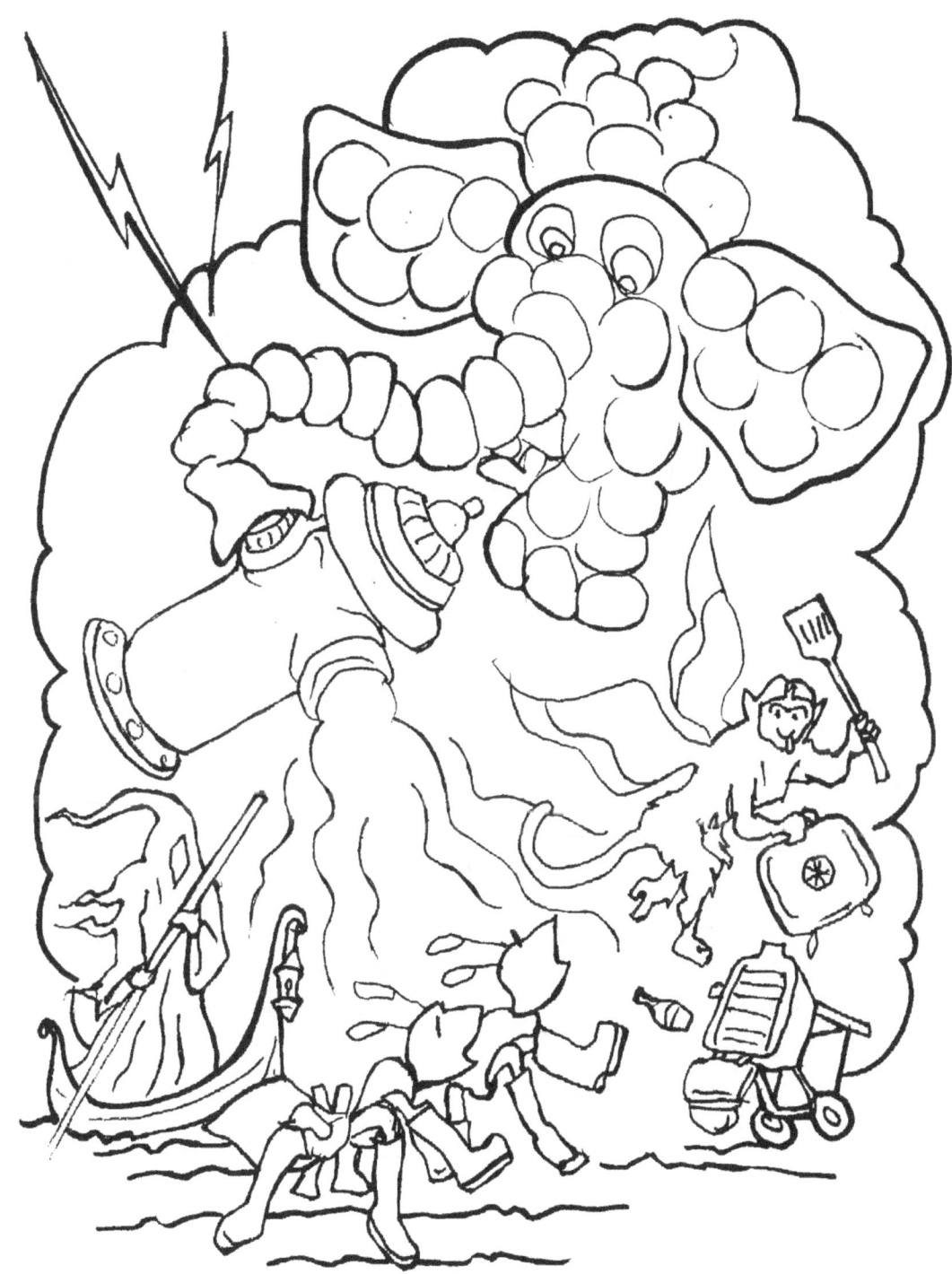

The sound and the fury

"Ooh," exclaimed Donna, who had been raised in this valley, "This is wonderful! You've never experienced a thunderstorm here before. Judging by those clouds, you're in for a real treat!"

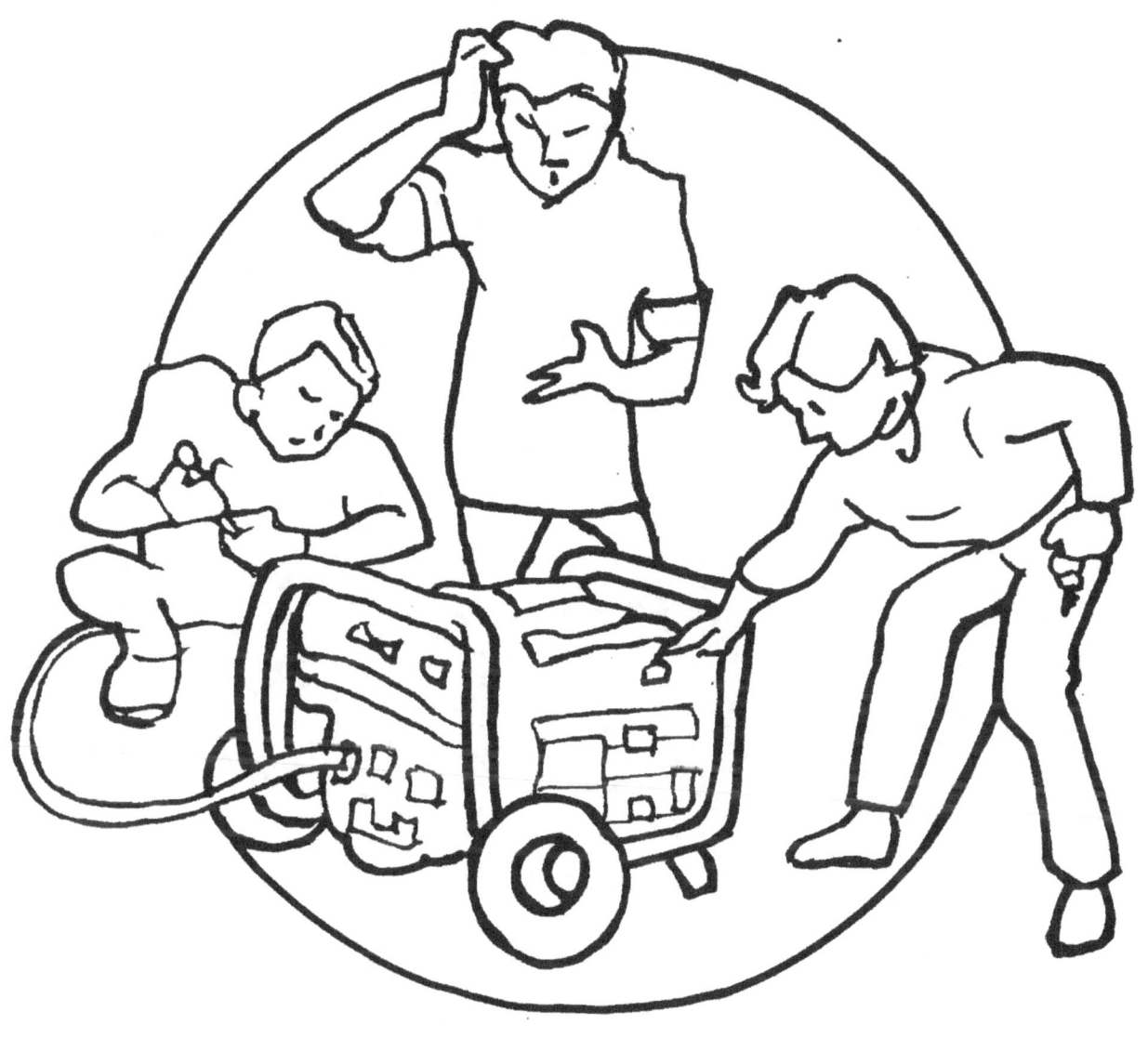

The three stooges.

"Thing is, we had never actually used this generator before. Had never actually used any generator before."

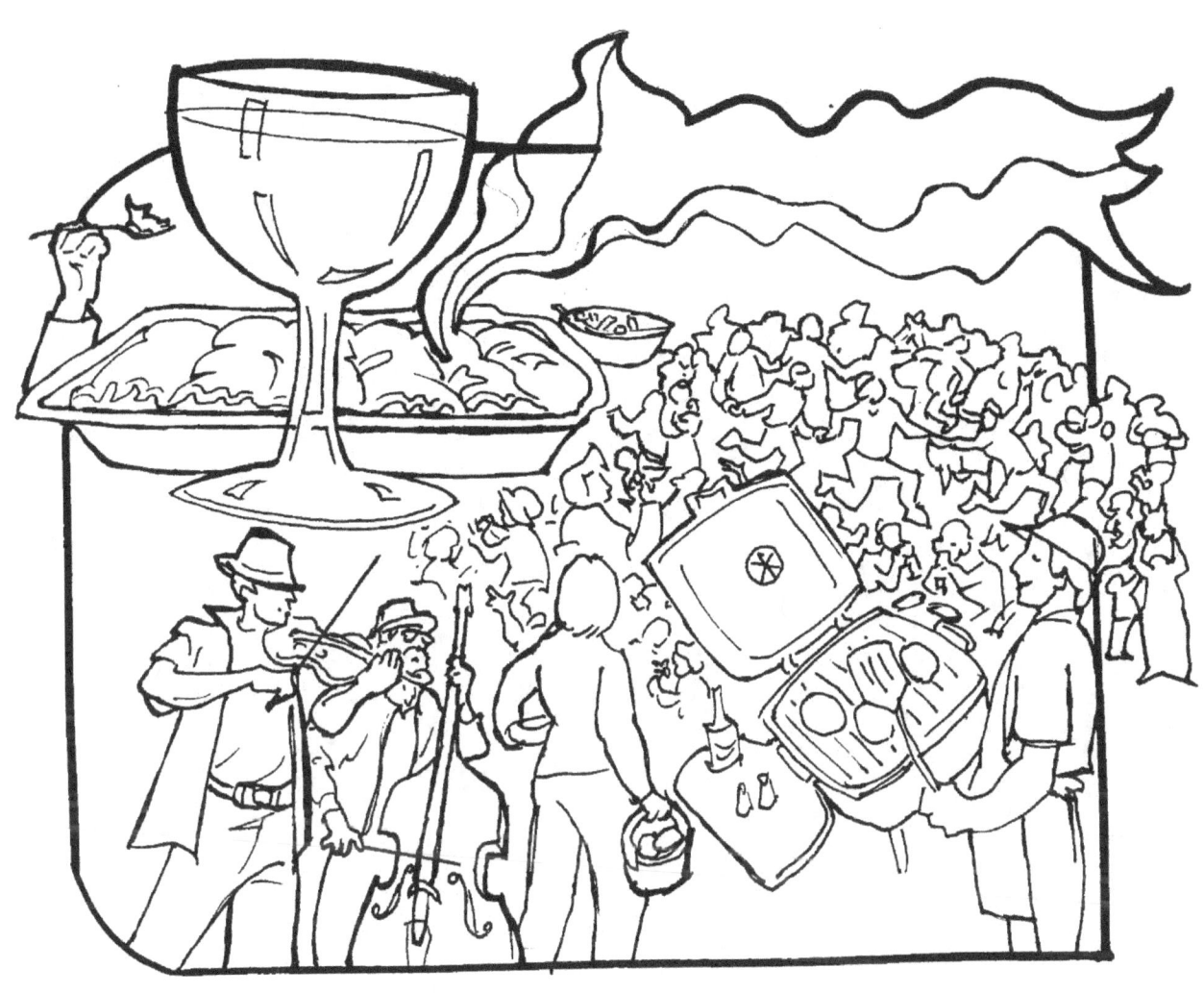

Bucolic soirees.

"In Bucolia, we celebrate life.
And sometimes it seems we live to celebrate."

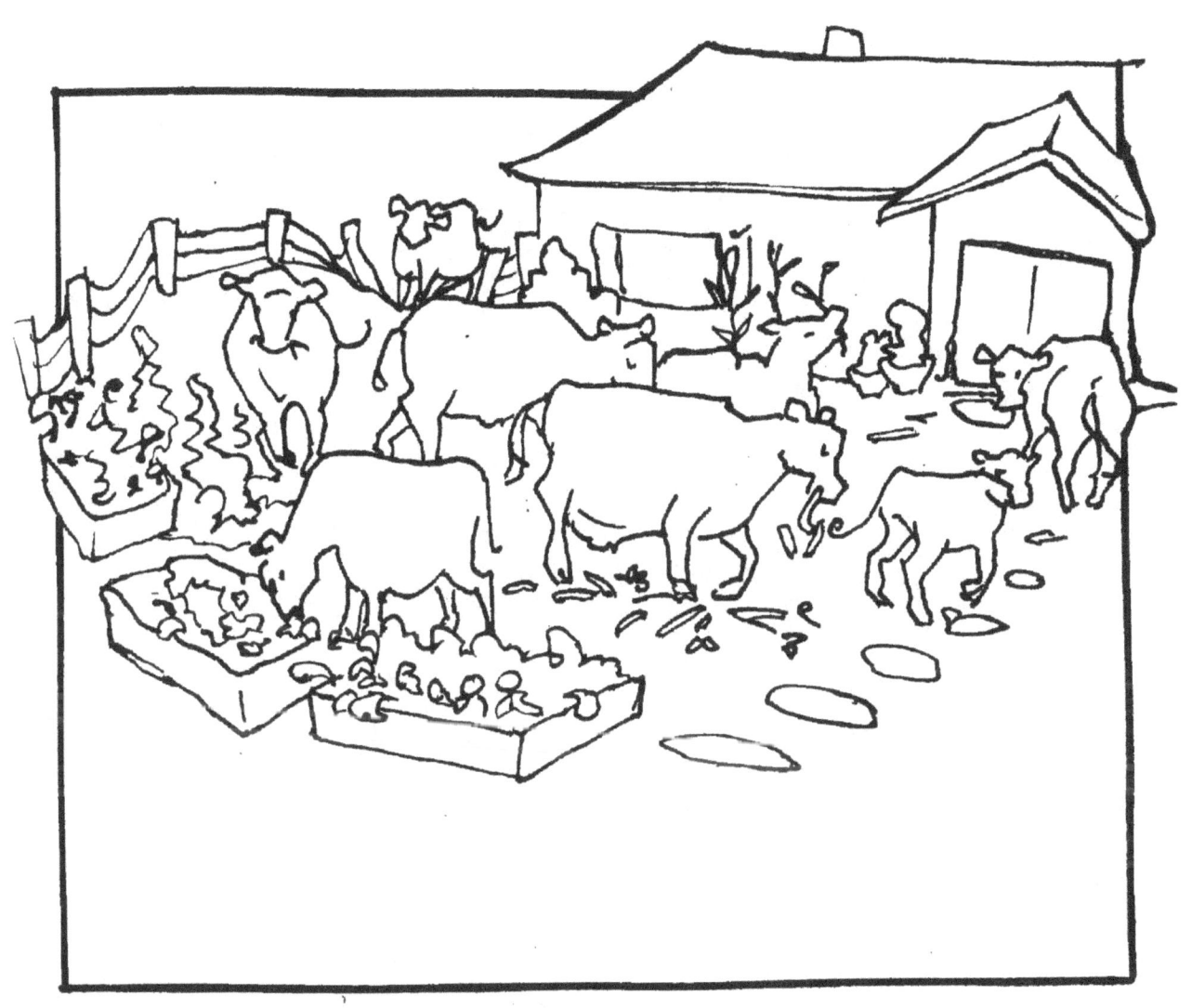

The great Independence Day bovine breakout.

"When it comes to celebrating, our bovine neighbors don't want to be left out. Or, apparently, in."

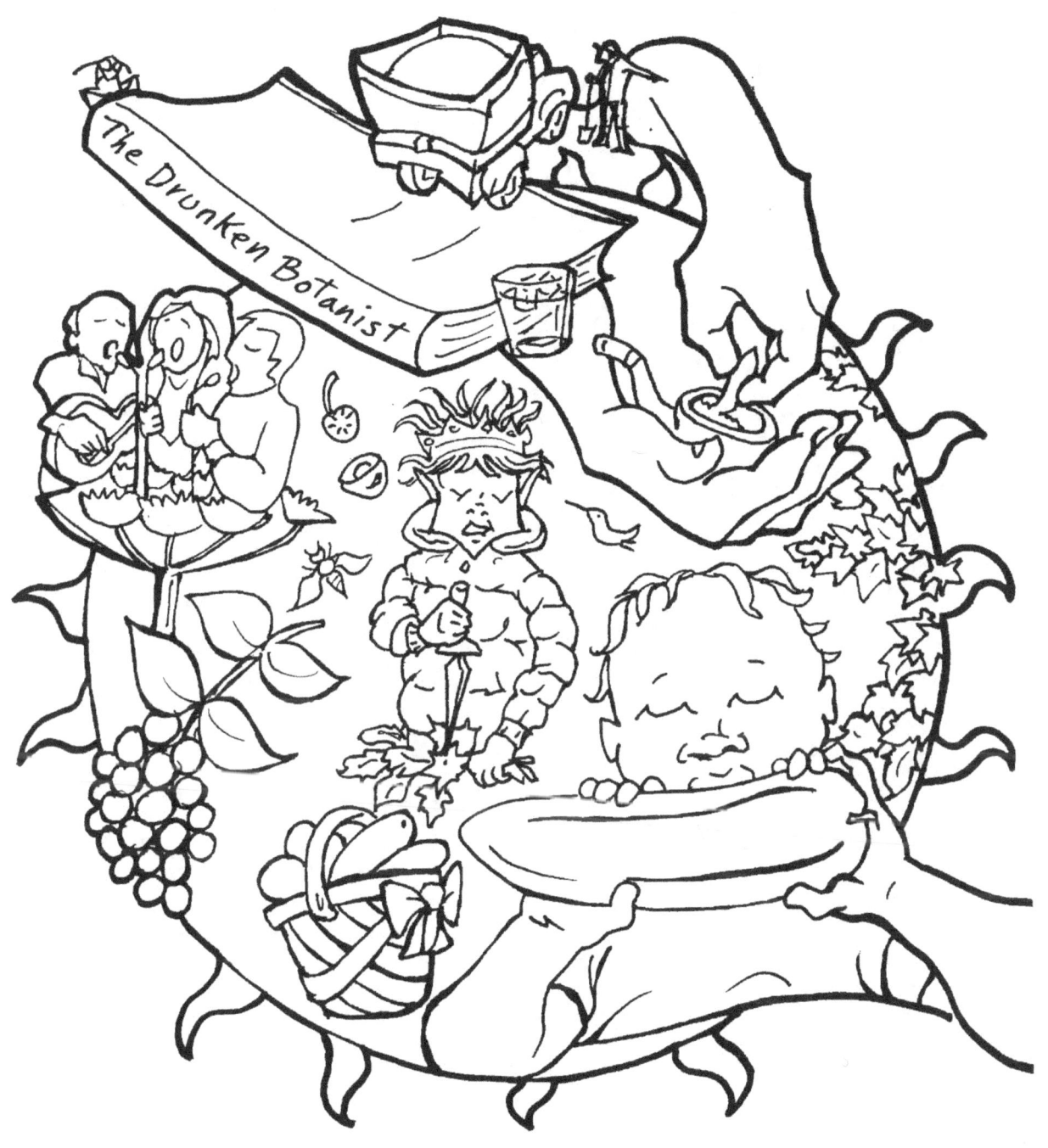

Blessed are the zone fives.

"Nowadays when we search for plants, the first thing we look for is, how hardy is this puppy? If it's a Zone 5 or lower, blessed be, it might just survive our hillside battleground."

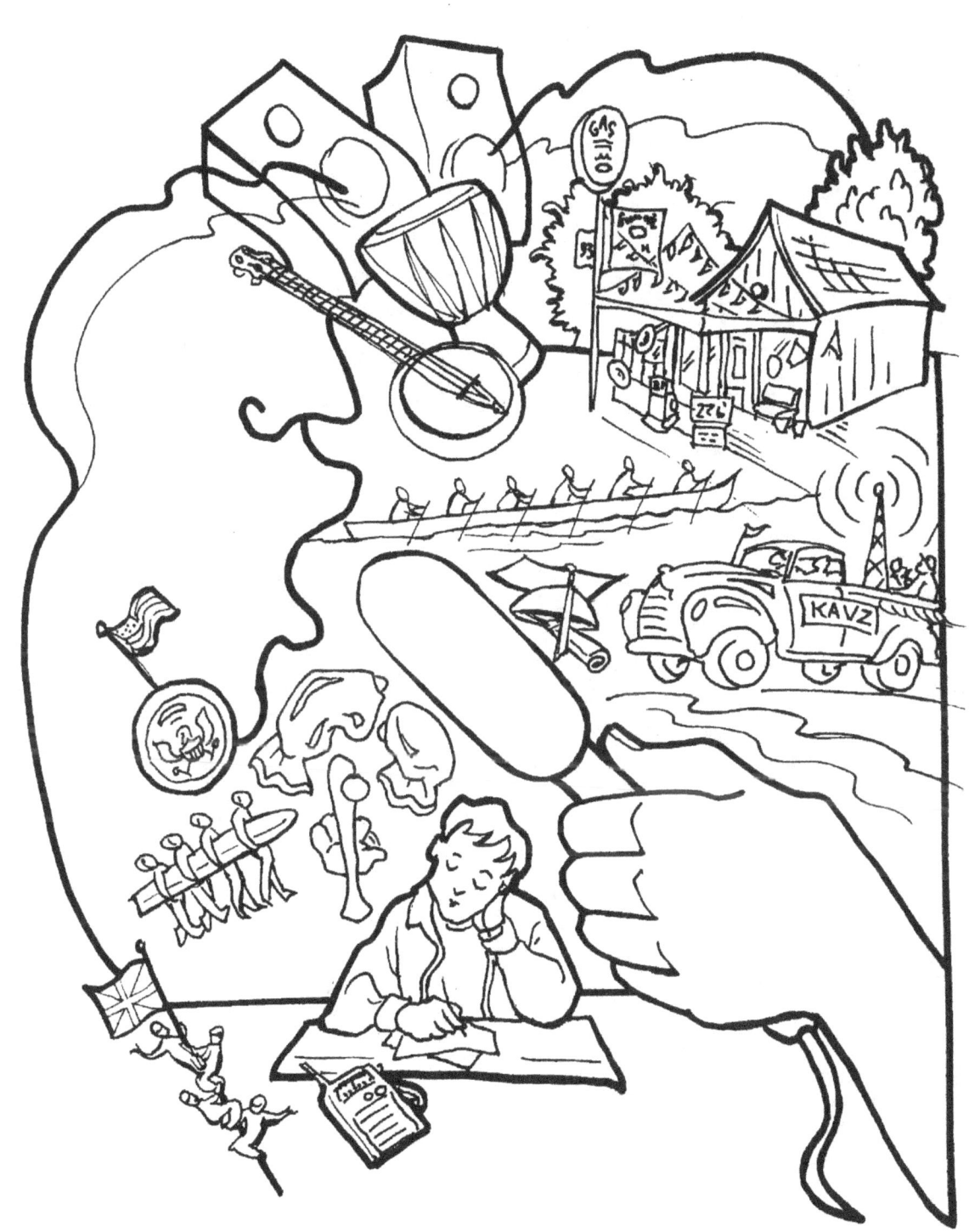

Radio Bucolia.

"I'm not going to tell you that Bucolia is a place where dreams can come true. But it is. Just trust me."

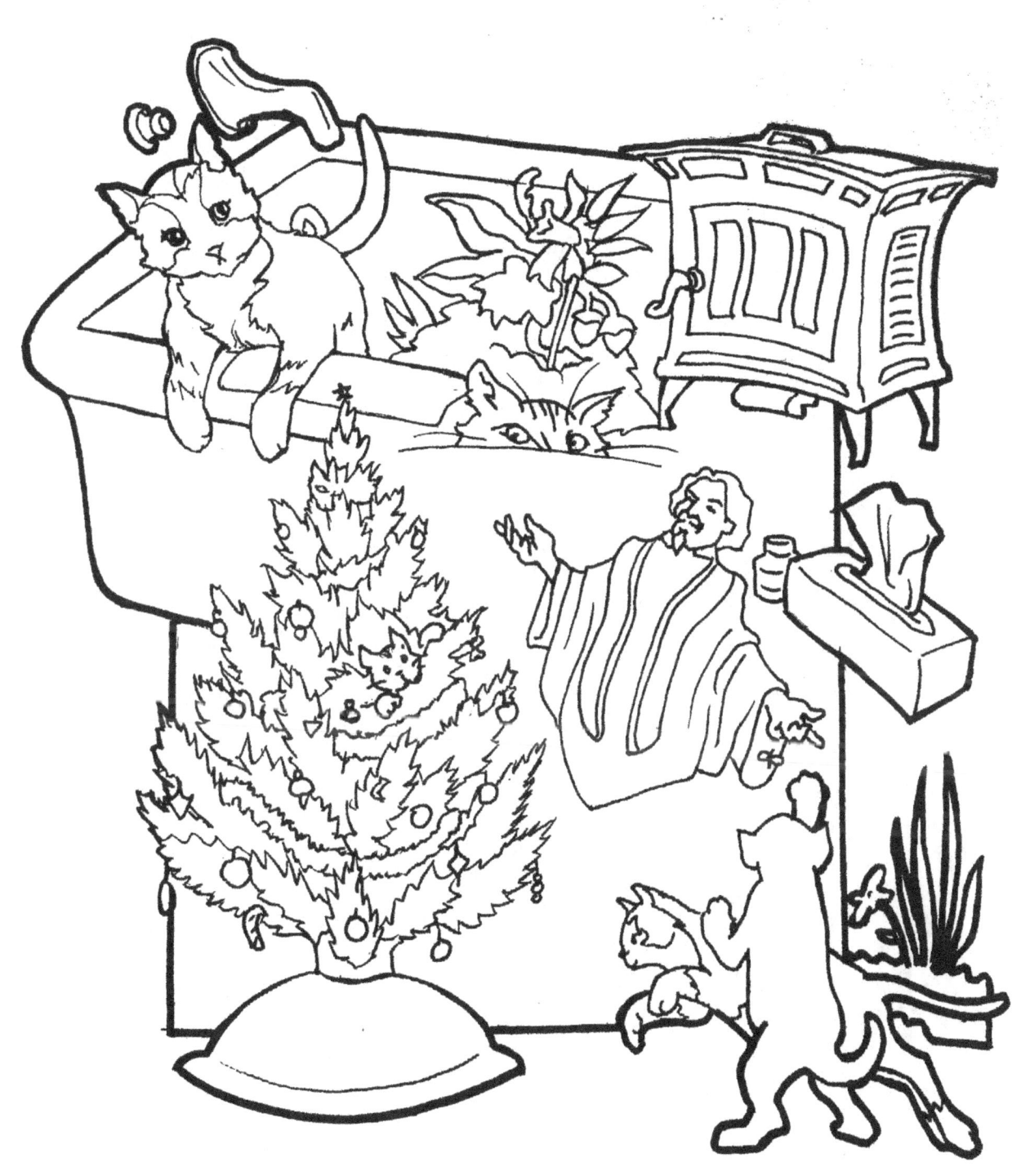

Rocky the cat.

"In some deep and mysterious way, we had become best buddies."

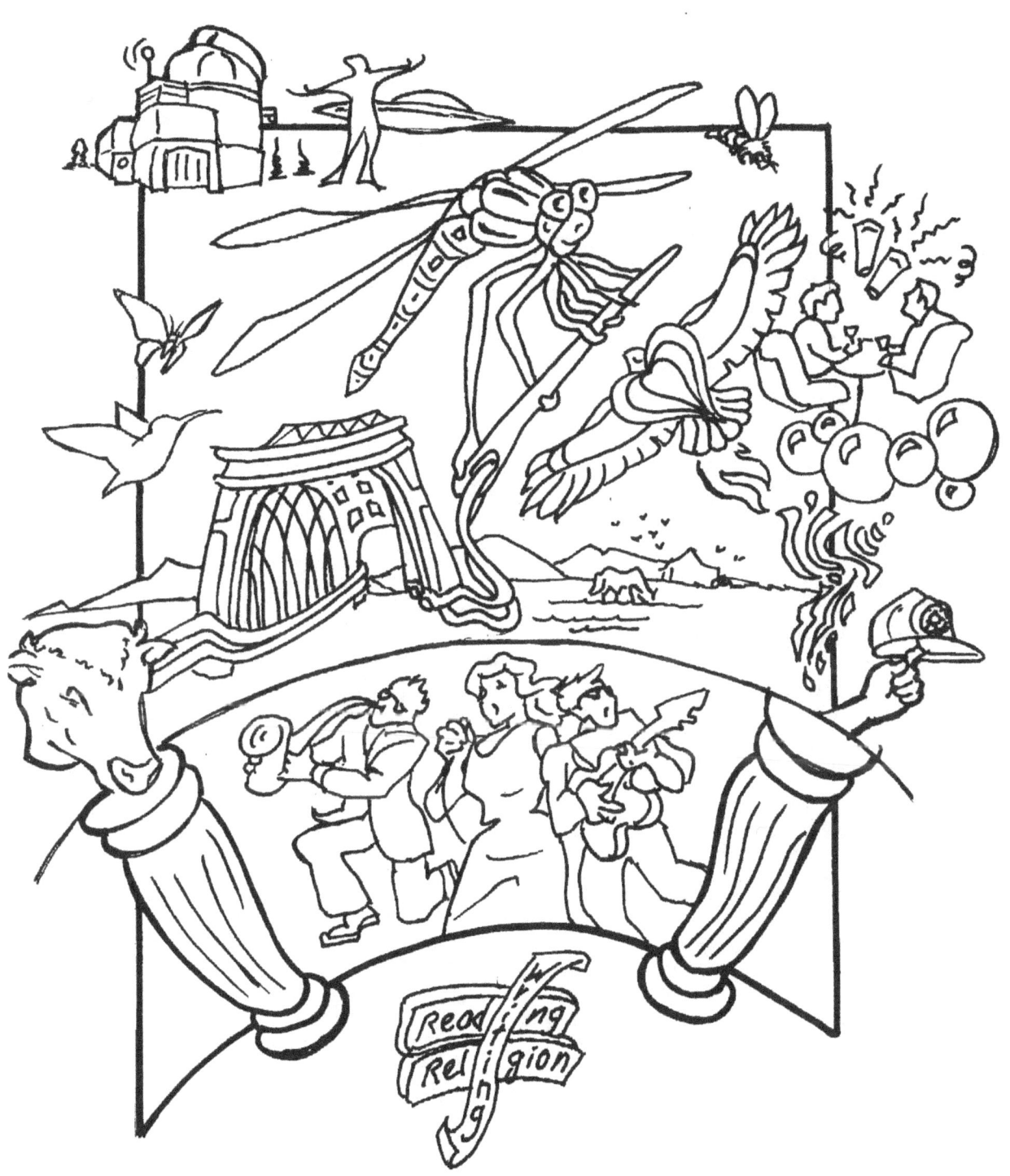

The pillar and the dragonfly.

"Bucolia is my pillar, and I am overcome by its support."

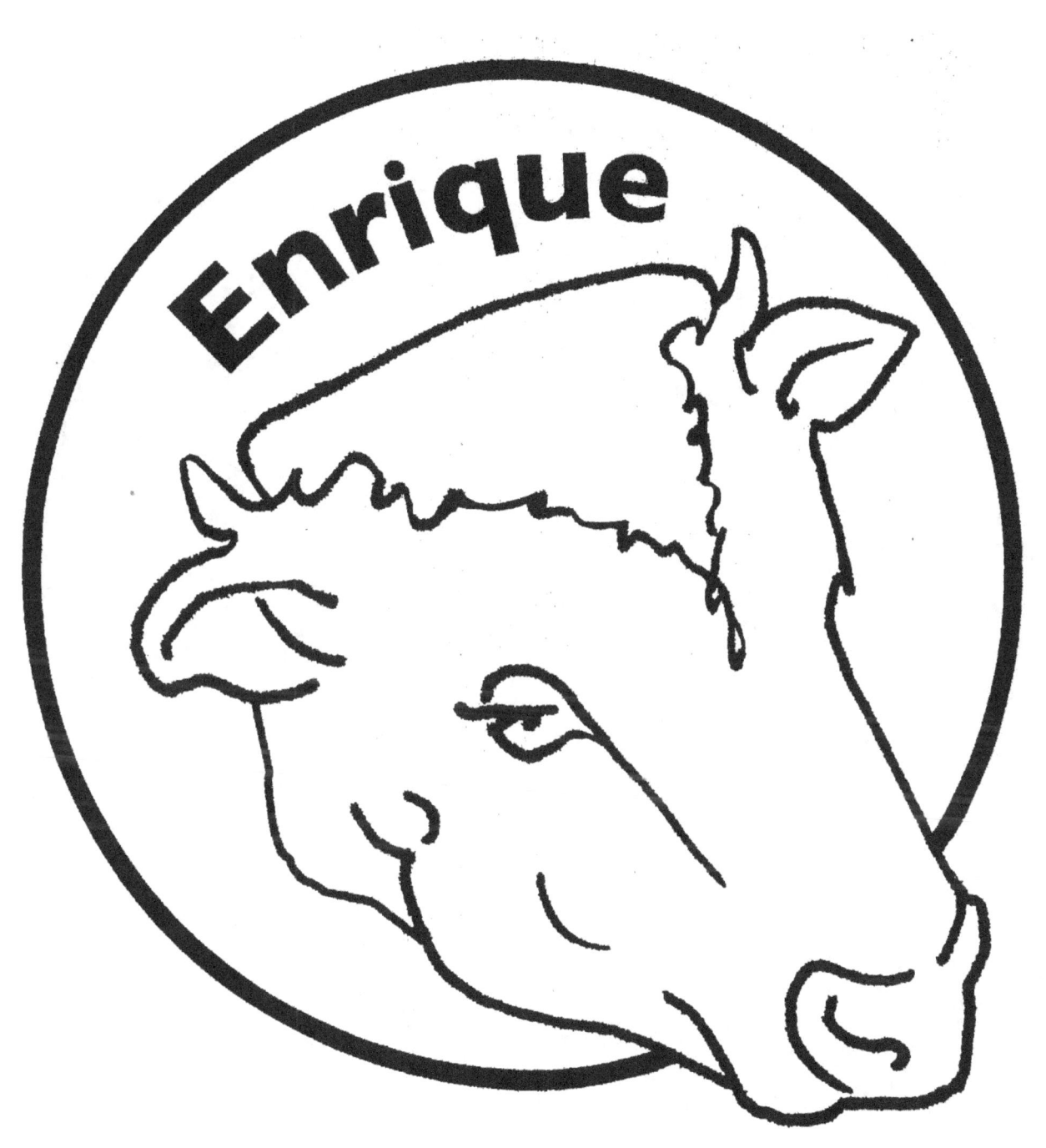

I sing the bovine electric.

"Watch the fields, my friends. They're out there. They're plotting. They're pooping. They're mooing in code."

Matthew Thuney: Mystified Scribe

Matthew wrote his first book, *The Egg*, when he was five years old. That is, if you can call a disjointed ten-page ramble about a mother dinosaur in search of her son (somehow attacking and sacking Chicago in the process) a book. Undeterred, he's been writing ever since.

The past 30 years or so have seen Matthew scribbling humor and human-interest pieces and crafting political blogs for consumption in the Pacific Northwest.

Besides the printed word, he has also shared a long-standing love affair with radio. In fact, he even attended the Columbia School of Broadcasting in San Francisco. While he truly enjoyed writing news copy and coming up with funny on-air segments, Matthew just didn't have the gift of gab back then to keep up the requisite DJ patter.

Spiritually, Matthew has always been a student and seeker. Early on, it looked as though his path would lead to the Episcopal ministry. Luckily for the Episcopal Church, that path turned into a 40-year detour.

But everything started falling into place when Matthew and his wife moved to the hinterlands of northwest Washington. Lo and behold, he rediscovered his journalistic muse, reporting on his bumbling attempts to adapt to country living; He rediscovered his radio voice when a small band of crazed volunteers fired up a community radio station; and he rediscovered his spiritual roots as new friends and neighbors approached Matthew to give eulogies and even preside over the marriages of loved ones.

Who'da thunk it?

Certainly not his long-suffering spouse, who thankfully remains at his side. Nor their puzzled families, who long ago gave up trying to figure Matthew out. Nor their two-and-a-half cats, who are always giving him quizzical looks that seem to say, "What the heck are you up to now?" or "Where's the treats?" or "Will you sit down already--I need a lap."

Ellen Clark: Ambient Artist

In her formative years Ellen studied fine art and business at the University of Utah, attended the Salt Lake Academy of Graphic and Fine Arts and attended Successful Artist School. She has more recently taken courses at Western Washington University, Shoreline College and accomplished Teaching Artist Training through the Washington State Arts Commission. For personal growth, she has a CTM through Toastmasters International and is a graduate of Excellence Northwest.

Always interested in the evolutionary trail of life, Ellen has been a fashion illustrator for a sporting goods company, cartographer for an engineering firm, product illustrator and copywriter for a nationwide drugstore, manager for several photography labs, and graphic designer for various ad agencies.

Recent work includes creating sequential art for stories and books, painting public murals, being lead scenic painter for a 1500 seat theatre, teaching art to children and adults and having an annual commission to festively paint the featured window at Bellingham's Cruise terminal.

She has been influenced by such artists as Peter Max, Maxfield Parrish, Vincent van Gogh, Aguste Rodin, Leonardo de Vinci and Buonarroti Michelangelo.

Settling into Bucolia is a new adventure, pack your things and come along. It's a colorful place!